If You Were Here
I Would Have Hands

IF YOU WERE HERE

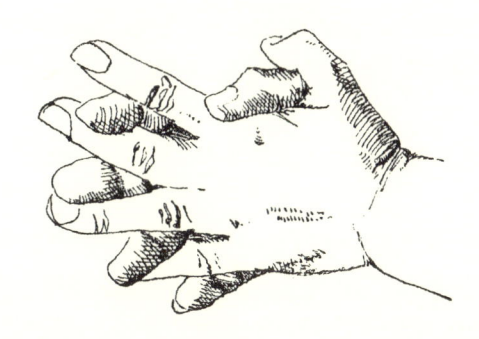

I WOULD HAVE HANDS

GARY HOLTHAUS

BROODING HERON PRESS · WALDRON ISLAND · 1999

Copyright © by Gary Holthaus

ISBN: 1-892275-03-1 Deluxe, signed
ISBN: 1-892275-04-X Trade Cloth
ISBN: 1-892275-05-8 Trade Paper

The author wishes to thank the National Endowment for the Arts for a grant which made the writing of many of these poems possible. Thanks also to Ted Chamberlin, Robert Hedin, and Gary Snyder for reading drafts of some of these poems.

Brooding Heron Press & Bindery
101 Bookmonger Road, Waldron Island, WA 98297

for Lauren

If You Were Here
I Would Have Hands

Someone Just Now

Someone just now
passing in the dusk
honked and waved.

I thought it was you.

A snow bunting leaped
straight up from the dark
as if entering the sun.

It was someone else.

The greeting was nice,
but here, in the rain,
a small bird's falling.

On the Road

Tonight you turn
in a wide motel bed

and I turn in ours at home
as if it were possible

to touch you, whisper
to you in the dark.

If You

were here,
pale as these sheets
against the dark,
I would have hands
to touch you, here
and here,
and a mouth

and you
would have hands
and a mouth,
and there would be
other parts to move
against the dark,
and warmth,

and we would be
warm and closer
than side by side,
finding ourselves
together
against the dark.

This Moment

I remember mostly your mouth,
soft with berries and words

taking me into this new country.
Blue lupine erect and open.

This clear air.

But I remember
other things as well—

My mouth against your face
wanting words to touch you,

these hands
wanting to touch you.

River

Your body, elastic,
stretches to greet me,
is rooted wherever you are,
travels with me
wherever I go.

Your voice reaches me
whenever I am myself.

My voice eases
into the river,
the black water's power
at the back of my throat
stretches my body toward you.

Now it is hard to remember
illusions of speed,
a vacancy in the voice,
the absence behind it,
the green distance it wishes
to narrow.

Your mouth opens,
takes my voice and the river's
over your tongue.
At the back of your throat
our words come together:

>Here,
>this is home.

Blouse

I wanted to tell you
earlier, this afternoon,
but didn't know how, quite,
and there wasn't time
at the time…

So I'll tell you now
what I thought then:

That's a beautiful blouse
you have on, pink as the pink
on the inside of your lips,
and never more beautiful than now:

You pulling it over your head
with all four of our hands,
letting it fall to the floor
in the hall.

Geometry

Such lines they say
are infinite:
this line in time that stretches
before us, and that other
tangent past which intercepts
the immediate arc of breast
or curve of spine.

Such lines are infinite
the mathematicians say,
patient, extending themselves...

But we know more,
know such lines to be too
easily broken, the curves
never closing quite—

until this angular intersection
where our lines meet,
this centering apex of thighs
where all our lines become one,
our own geometry of love.

Now I

who have not laid my life
on line for years
nor kept at things
that make me strong
think of you
and put my life at stake
once more

and think of spaces
you create—
that dark and female
emptiness which I
would now and again
(and again and again) fill—

Words

I take these words in both my hands,
that they might touch you
as my hands touch you,
moving lightly, your whole body
rising under my words, my hands.

I place these words upon my lips,
my lips moving softly against your face,
brushing your hair, filling
your eyes, your ears, your mouth
with my words…

I keep these words
at the front of my tongue, my tongue
planting my words in you like seeds:
they will blossom, their colors
burst inside our mutual darkness.

The unknown words we will yet create
flood inside us, like this sunlight
flooding over these white sheets,
this glistening sheen on your skin.

Hands

Sometimes, I swear,
I believe my hands
are the seat of memory,

in their palms and fingers
so much of what I know
of you is held.

I look at my hands,
see you lift yourself
over me again,

the fall you turned
your breasts loose to fill
the curving fingers of desire.

All that feeling for you
made visible again
here, in these hands

opening as they reach
to touch you, turning
as you turn to me…

New Year

Awakened by stillness
you draw back the curtains,
watch the yard slowly descend
into a white and trackless cover.

Your voice so soft
I lean forward to listen;
my voice, a question
you cannot answer.

Together
we watch the still snow
gather the year.

Summer

My voice enters you
slowly as seasons
speaking in tongues.

Tendons stretch
the skin of your throat;
we tremble at a word.

You open the window,
return to the bed.
White curtains plume.

Canyon Voice

This canyon is so far
from any trails
no man has seen it,

so narrow and deep in the Beartooths,
after seventy million years of effort
the exquisite sun has yet to reach bottom.

The voice of this canyon is lightning,
wide-eyed crescendo of color
and darkness opaque to every eye.

From a cleft in the canyon wall
the voice of a bird ignites the silence,
quick stabs of beak, preening the thunder.

My voice and the canyon's
call you to join us, promise you
light enough to find us.

You are the river on the canyon floor.
I slide into you; you take my life
jolting through rapids, slamming against rocks.

I stammer, cry out, give myself up
to the current, spin in the eddies,
drenched but not drowning.

Summit Lake

Knowing the sudden darkness
after the candle is out
will not take these mountains far,

I sleep between you and the cattails,
light wind adrift in the pines,
a few thin cirrus hazing the moon.

The return of light will show you
curling beside me still,
sunlit breast shadowed by my hand.

West of the Bighorns

Here is the land beyond rivers,
what will be left, scarred and forever
when we are gone and the sun returns.

Dry ribs arc up from the hard red
hide of a cow, dead in the desert
but months. Chalk white skull
stares from the sage.

I turn to you, cool stream
in the desert, light in my arms.
In all this space, yours
the only voice in our solitude
healing the scars, scooping up
peace with your hands.

Mesa Trail

Between the tender light rising
and the foothills' shadow falling
we walk the curve of coming night.

Mule deer watch, ears up,
alert but undisturbed, our
downwind presence watching them.

We come down in growing strength,
the moon's white face,
sky blue as a gunbarrel,

to eat with the moon,
no need for extra light
or anything artificial.

My hand drops across the table,
open to your hand
turning up to mine.

Fraser Meadows Pond

These geese tilt
all the way from Canada

to slide crosswind and settle
here in mid-October light.

On days like this, the wind
a woman's voice from long ago,

the heart tilts to find
its space in light and air.

Whatever grace we've grown
we use to spill our wings

and set ourselves to settle here
at home on buoyant days.

Voice on the Clear Air

My voice on the clear air
is autumn.

Days shorten at a word
mountains go dark, sky flares.

You take the high country
in stride, body light and agile

hiding the pain inside.
Our voices together

free us from longing
bring us no injury

promise nothing.

Downslope I wait in the pines

hoping you will come with me.
Together we will ease into winter

lift our faces to the first snow
now falling to uneasy rest on our arms.

We will put arms and warmth
around one another,

fend off the cold with laughter.
At the far edge of our voices

dark pods of lupine burst
their seeds drop,

open to
the promise of color.

North Wind

We speak of trees.
Their leaves carry
our voices back to us.

All through the forest
our words tear loose,
spin down on the wind.

We scuff through them
kicking up dust,
discovering color.

We talk of rivers,
how ice appears now,
mornings, along the edges;

how many words
are swept downstream, lost
in the flow of language.

My voice grows older,
querulous and quarrelsome,
turns stoney.

Your voice is water,
rounds the sharp corners,
smooths the rough edges.

Your words carry me
erect and bobbing
lift me as I go under.

Tracks

We have come far
to reach this place,
have far to go.

Beyond this curve of hill
the ocean's track,
behind these clouds

stars track, and more—
heart's road rising
through this grass, heading home.

THREE HUNDRED copies of this book were printed during an atypical Pacific Northwest summer: clouds, rain, and very little sun. Twenty-six were printed on Rives Lightweight, lettered A-Z, signed by the poet, printer, binder, and artist, and bound by hand into cloth and paper over boards. The remaining copies were printed on Mohawk Superfine and sewn into paper wrappers or hand bound into full cloth over boards. The text type is Lutetia, set by hand; title page display is Perpetua Titling. The original art work is by Julie Loyd. The pages were fed through a 1920 treadle-operated C & P platen press, while the printer blessed the mild temperatures as well as visiting with friends from Utah who relieved the routine and brightened the days. After 17 years of doing without, the publishers celebrated getting cold *and* hot running water into their home, and adopted their son's cat, Hayduke, when Lonnie left the island to try his hand at living in the wide world.